I0756331

FINISHING LINE PRESS
www.finishinglinepress.com

The Woods ~ Trails & Tangents

poems by

Stan Winarski

Finishing Line Press
Georgetown, Kentucky

The Woods ~
Trails & Tangents

ISBN 979-8-89990-486-8 First Edition

ACKNOWLEDGMENTS

I am grateful to the organizers and judges of the 2025 Finishing Line Press Open Chapbook Competition for selecting this collection and bringing these poems into the world.

Special thanks to *The Solitary Plover* and *WFOP Calendar*, who first gave my poems voice.

Heartfelt acknowledgment to the editors of *Bramble* and *Landward: Readings of Place and Season*, where versions of poems from this collection first appeared.

To my wife, Mary Kay, for her patient forbearance of my writing late into the night, sometimes until early morning, and at times all day long—this book would not exist without your understanding and support.

To Bill and Bernice Fairman (my Farmer Bill and Bernie), whose generous sale of forty acres to my father provided the foundation for these woodland observations and imaginings.

To my father, who loved this land every bit as much as I do.

To Kelly, who introduced me to the Wisconsin Fellowship of Poets.

To Theodor Seuss Geisel, Ogden Nash, and my mother for first instilling in me the love of words and rhyme.

And to the many friends and fellow writers who offered encouragement along the way—my thanks.

Publisher: Leah Huete de Maines
Editor: Christen Kincaid
Cover Art: Stan Winarski
Author Photo: Katie Fromstein Photography
Cover Design: Elizabeth Maines McCleavy

Order online: www.finishinglinepress.com
also available on amazon.com

Author inquiries and mail orders:
Finishing Line Press
PO Box 1626
Georgetown, Kentucky 40324
USA

Contents

Autumn Clear

Autumn clear,
chipmunk and I,
with dusking near,
sat eye to eye.
It on wind snap,
me on my stand,
with pad in lap
and pen in hand.
Both frozen still,
without a blink.
Quite long, I think,
prolonged until…
Did broken glance
or tiny twitch
the spell unstitch
and break our trance?
'Twas it or me
caused it to flee?
How could I know
which one was so?
Think I to blame.
I let it lay.
As clear blurred gray,
deep shadows came.
The gift of woods
to watch and wait,
no bad or good—
no pending fates.
With end of light
and coming night,
such inner calm—
my autumn's balm.

This Hour

For today—this hour
Sit on the fallen oak,
Watch for the sake of watching,
But not reflecting—

The forest stands before you.
Don't interfere by thinking—
Make no "like" or "as."
Intentions might disrupt
This fragile moment.

Let the chickadee flit.
Let the ferns be ferns.
Be without—
            —Context—
            —Explanation—

Save words for another day,
Let being still—be enough.

Two Boulders in Repose

In woods I know two sibling boulders stand
Apart from knolls and slopes of northern clime
So long at rest since God's almighty hand
Delivered them before the birth of time.

Primeval litter strewn from glacier flow
That random-scattered rock like windswept seed
Across the frozen landscape long ago
Then melted, leaving mountain remnant freed.

O, silent soul of age-old granite gray
Unchanged by pass of season or of year
Immune to mortal's tenement of clay
Succumb so slow from winter's wrath severe.

When I a lad was lost in baleful wood
Disheartened by a panic-filled discord
I'd seek the place where in repose they stood
For then the compass points would be restored.

Near six feet tall with narrow space between
A shelter safe from winter's raging storm
For lighted fire tiny yet serene
Enough to make both soul and body warm.

I've braced my hands against its massive weight
And felt a graveled sound, an ancient groan
Within my mind did thoughts reverberate
Or were they words that had their source in stone?

Perhaps a life lived out at epoch pace,
Unheard its breath, each hundred thousand years,
And every era's pulse beat without trace,
Forever silence absent joy and tears.

Then know the mortal fleeting of my soul
For yesterday, I was, but boy at dawn
But millstones take their heavy gristing toll
Now vesper-like my life is nearly gone

Tomorrowed soon my flesh to dust returns,
No graveyard tombstone chiseled name and date.
Between the two I'll wait in the eterne
As granite slowly shares a common fate.

NW¼NW¼ of Section 12, Township 37 North, Range 8 West, Sawyer County, Wisconsin

Broadcast on Landward with Catherine Young, 91.9 FM WDRT, December 2025

Daybreak

awake
day breaks
and makes
dawn's ink
of pink,
i think—
it's true
the hue
not blue—
light sent
then bent
fragment—
ahead
it spread
and bled—
i stayed
and bade
the fade

Come Walk with Me

Come walk with me along the lake—
its secrets delicate and grand.
Come listen to the whitecaps break,
touch limestone coarse worn into sand.

Red cedars, clustered, guard the way
and banish thoughts of time and place
with tangled snare of roots that lay
on humus black to slow our pace.

Light falls through leaves of braided jade—
like love it brightens bloom by chance
but shrouds some beauty in dim shade
observed through moment's random glance.

Look high onto the jagged bluff
by ancient glaciers torn and hewn,
smooth facets scoured yet edges rough
with shadowed cave and crevice strewn.

Horizon wide of blue on blue
by endless waves the sky is worn
to color of a lighter hue—
familiar denim stressed and torn.

Hear breeze recite its lonesome rhyme,
and in response waves fall and swell.
The shoreline flowers sway in time,
entranced by nature's soothing spell.

Drink in the day, and feel its peace—
converge with land and endless sky.
In nature's balm find sweet release.
Your stress, like gulls, on thermals fly.

Fall Markers

fresh acorn carpet
feet crush some, others eaten
one roots, grows ancient

golden ferns at rest
their greenness gone for season
cairns of the trail

leaves flutter earthward
an ochre-colored rainbow
against clear blue sky

Hunting Blind

There is a hunting blind I know
where white pines long have stood—
a place to see 'round and below
from ridge above the wood.

I've stared afar like bird of prey
and listened with my eyes
for tiny tell that might betray
a forested disguise.

This morn the scene is filled with gray—
low settled mist of clouds.
The landscape has been washed away
by icy frozen shroud.

The world a blurry monochrome
with sodden kind of chill—
my thoughts begin to turn to poem
as if by nature's will.

Is quiet simply sound stripped bare?
Is emptiness a song?
It seems to me a kind of prayer—
be still and listen long.

The forest unearths many things,
some meanings hidden deep—
accept the gift that silence brings.
Its secret—yours to keep.

Old Boots

These boots I've worn for 30 years
with rubber stitched to leather.
My old familiar hunting gear
for stormy winter weather.

The uppers soft from hand-rubbed grease,
to soften and to seal.
Yet age has shaped with frown and crease
to warm accustomed feel.

The soles have simple zig-zag tread
in woods I've known as mine.
On virgin snow they've often led
and later served as sign.

They've sixteen eyes that lace up tight.
Their packs are dense and warm.
They fit my low-arched soles just right
with seasoned kind of charm.

I've worn them in a blizzard harsh
'til toes ached fierce with pain.
I've drenched them in a frozen marsh
then walked down logging lane.

An unused pair now two years old,
of Gore-Tex micro woven blend,
they may be best in wet and cold,
but can't replace my long-time friend.

Snowshoeing at Homestead

Today between harsh winter storms,
when wind was calm, and sun was warm,
put on my gloves, put on my hat,
put on my snowshoes as I sat.

To trek at Homestead, my dear park
I picked my trail and set my mark.
The trail'd been forged by one or two,
on virgin snow—the lucky few.

Light breath, high spirits filled my day,
all worried thoughts somehow at bay.
Tree limbs bowed low with heavy snow
and often made my going slow.

The air was filled with pine scent rich,
enchantment of fae florist witch.
My arms and legs found rhythmed pace,
as I strode on with gliding grace.

Trail whispered "hush" as I strode by,
then from above crow's welcome cry,
at my parole from stifling jail,
as I found bliss on snowshoe trail.

Done at Dusk

Shadows lengthen and sunlight thins.
I sit in the deepening darkness.
Pleased by the loss of day.
Joyful at being done.
Alone in thought.
Breathing.

The Crows' Lament

Bleak winter morn in stand of birch,
from field and forest gathered crows
in twos and threes began to perch,
as branches filled, laments arose.

On treetop high lit Barren Lord
who shared their discontented plight.
Might Goddess Nature soothe this horde?
"Aloft!" he cried. "Comrades, take flight!"

Her stateroom stood midst grove of pines,
hewn granite boulder as a throne.
A nimbus glowed—Eden Divine.
Entreating crows begged plaints be known.

"O Mistress Mother, lift our curse.
Please let us fly on satin wing,
transform our brazen cry to verse
that we like other birds may sing."

"O Goddess Earth, aloud we pray,
transfigure black to color bright,
a harbinger of peaceful day,
no longer omen of the night."

She pondered them with grace-filled eyes
like sunshine, mercy filled her heart.
For long She'd known their mournful cries
"I've loved thee always as thou art."

"O dearest ones, I've heard your cant.
Eat only seed and berry fresh.
Your supplication I shall grant
if you abstain from fallen flesh."

The murdered crows in anger cawed,
their hearts like darkest mines of coal.
For She unmasked their carnal god
whose bloodlust stained their inmost souls.

Rocks and Ravens

Imagine
rocks dreaming of wings—
groundedness taking flight,
leaving earth and gravity below;
no longer material, but ethereal.
Having never known dizzy or giddy,
they float—on thermals—
naming all they see below,
like Adam in his Eden.
Horizons and dimensions broadening,
eons transforming into infinites.
Flying homeward—never to return.
Their past becoming so far away.

Imagine
ravens seeking beauty—
aspiring to be Renoirs and Rodins—
ascending to Grandmaster.
They wing-brush birch pastels,
talon-sculpt granite Davids.
Their nests woven tapestries,
gladly forsaking conspiracies
for enlightened expression
created both as penance for sins
and as testimony to redemption.
Transcending ancient stigmas—
no longer harbingers of death,
but artists of light.

Previously published in Bramble, Winter/Spring, 2025

Dear Elizabeth Bishop,

I pause at your woodland's edge.
Oh, how its heart beckons—
its dappled light—
and sinuous swaying.

Hesitantly—I step inward.
The footing uncertain—
with tree falls and animal burrows—
I must pause to contemplate.

How lovely its undulations!
Hillocks and hollows
gracefully rise and fall
as contoured pentameter.

Shadows limit my vision—
but in the foreground
sedge and fern commingle
in a verdant menagerie.

Deeper I wander—
until I am lost
without a palindrome
to retrace my steps.

Sighing, I close my eyes—
Though my trek is incomplete,
I take one glance back—
as I return to the margin.

Shared Secret

Forty years—
I have walked these woods.
Hills and hollows remain steadfast
but gone are the stable rhythms
of snow and rain.
Vindictive droughts, manic rains
wither and blight foliage
and strain the water table.
Spring unfolds earlier,
fall migrates later.
Summer scorches more harshly,
winter storms howl less often,
but more voraciously.
The canopy, understory,
resistant to change
struggle to acclimate.

I stand amidst this ecosystem—
on the cusp of a knoll
near my familiar cairn marker—
a domed boulder with patchwork
of granite gray and moss green,
evoking Earth itself.
Before entering deeper
I pause to center myself,
sighing and briefly closing my eyes.
As I do, a crow caws
and poplar leaves rustle in utter calm.
When I reopen them, nothing is familiar.

I find myself in a foreign universe
with soft footing of spongy peat.
Above me strands of luminescent green
spiral skyward like interwoven chromosomes
forming intricate lattices.

Pinecone spores tether like tiny parachutes.
Amidst this molecular-like maze, shorter tendrils
form an almost impassable cellulose bramble.
I am unable to absorb such exoticness.
Am I first witness to such alien terrain?

Furthering my disorientation,
ahead wanders an obese eight-legged worm
lumbering like a drunken bear—
translucent—eyeless, with a black hole gape.
Before I can process this eerie sight,
another aberration appears—
A herky-jerky torpedo—
antenna as long as its body
rocketing sunward then skydiving earthward,
landing on its launch point and scurrying off,
leaving dander dust and me wondering—

There is no inkling of a trail.
No sun discerning East from West.
All is thicket, all is dense.
Yet not all is as it would seem.
Verdant is drier, lithe more stiff
than at first glance.
Fronds droop and leaves brown—
stressed like the woods I left.
微型陰影 Wéixíng yīnyǐng
I pass by a small hollow—
remnant of a vernal pool,
dried vegetation encircles—
a chalky emptiness within.
Skeletons of tiny snails lay scattered.
A smaller ecosystem—barren.
I gather the shells into my palm,
forming a tiny graveyard.

Overcome by the fragility
a tear falls into the basin.
As I wipe my eyes, a crow caws—
the leaves rustle despite the calm—
and I have been returned to the cusp
where I once stood.
Again, I am disoriented
despite my familiar spot
but with a new outlook.

From woodland path to microbe realm
I've seen how fine are forest threads—
woven on a loom of earth's climate.
I cannot change our planet's course—
One man—mid bed of moss.
Yet my footprints leave imprints
larger than I conceive.
So lightly I shall try to tread
respecting earth by thinking small
with gentle steps for fragile home.

微型陰影 *Miniature Shadow*

Friend of Wood

I've come to sit here many years
Among the oaks and pines,
With oft a question, "why's it so?"
The woodland forms a focus clear,
Perhaps I'll draft some lines,
Or just observe what day bestows.

The forty acres, give or take,
Were handed down to me.
I've spared it both the axe and saw,
Let God or age the windfalls make,
It's best to let it be,
Subject alone to nature's laws.
Some moments linger light on air,
Then withered fall like leaves,
Reposing on a shaded hill.

What right have I to daydream there?
But friend am I, no thief,
Who loves enigma of the still.
'Tis I who come and listens long,
Who knows each cleft and knoll,
And quiet sits and leaves no sign,
Who hears the lyrics of earth's song,
The tune of wooded soul,
And seeks to make my psalms align.

Winter Vigil

When snow through silent forest falls,
and winter blows its frozen kiss,
rich autumn hues long taken flight,
the earth is brushed with wedding white.
My heart rests in a tranquil bliss,
like stillness after winter squall.

Dull pewter clouds past treeline roll,
their surly temper tantrum still.
A southern sun, with artist hand
frosts treetops high with golden band.
As I look down atop the hill,
the twinkling snow illumes my soul.

Light shadows muted blue on gray
upon the silent scene are cast.
They cover hill and hollow deep,
blanket for newborn fast asleep.
My time to sit and dream now past,
old leather boots will know the way.

Down logging trail I now descend
through powders soft with shuffled gait,
hips moving slowly, ankles ache.
In moon's bright glow drifts lone snowflake,
fades into darkness—the hour late,
a fitting close to vigil's end.

Fall

The smoke of leaves burning
and its acrid twinge in my nostrils.
Marigolds blooming in a last gasp frenzy
near molding tomato vines.
A prescient wind
before fall's inevitable decay.
The sun having faded summer,
has turned on itself.
Windfall apples spoiling
under their mothers' arms.
Rich Wisconsin soil tilled to sleep;
aromatic, dank, and pungent.
The first scent of recognition
that what was, has ended.
All melded on a breeze which will not stay.

Some need their spring scented utopias
with lilacs and first grass cuttings.
Others, the lavender and fresh dill
of a summer paradise.

I pray my heaven smells like fall.

Previously published in 2024 Wisconsin Poets' Calendar

The Nature of Solitude

In northern clime a wooded knoll,
to passerby no second thought,
a silent and secluded stand
to survey distant untamed ground,
and make a way with little sound.
Its emptiness so clear at hand,
and packing as it were I brought
just ambling heart and pensive soul.

This harshly barren place, it's true,
no place for contemplative mood.
The woods appear uncanny still
but earth has dug and thrown its own,
ripped massive oak, heaved giant stone—
it's here I ponder *was* and *will*
the nature of true solitude—
of infinite, a point of view.

November landscape cold and bare—
true wildness, an untamed place.
Long fallen tree for my repose,
where only my own breath is heard.
This copse transcends the written word,
an ancient type of cryptic prose
with wild, ragged sense of grace,
untouched by plow or saw, so rare.

Have sound and stirring fearful flown
or fallen to the ground like leaves?
Does silence creep through forest floor
and softly flood the woods with calm,
its incense sweet, new winter's balm?
This solitude—mind's open door
where thoughts and dreams together weave
and we release claimed truth we've known.

Mortality & Blueberries

Fresh wild blueberries,
succulent tiny blessings,
clustered and cloistered,
like wilderness monasteries,
in the Lake of the Clouds terrace.
Only foolish or brave fingers
dare pilfer from black bear owners.

It has been many blue summers
since I last crushed them
between my tongue and palate
and felt their berry-burst monsoon,
far more intense
than their cultivated cousins—
the market's mimic wannaberries.

The wild ones hide in pine barrens.
I no longer venture there.
Fewer berry seasons remain for me,
and they may never linger on my tongue again.
Alas, life is filled with losses,
but also with tart memories.

What Is

Crow I

crisp wooded silence
punctuated by a crow
seeking to own it

Crow II

crisp wooded silence
broken by a crow's keening
Which is lonelier

Dragon I

windfall dragons lurk
carnage on a fall forest
plot covert revenge

Dragon II

windfall dragons lurk
tripping inattentive steps
ankle snaps, breath gasps

My Poem Has a Mosquito in It

Despite the heavy rains of late,
we set out for remote trailhead,
of rocky knoll and washed-out kame,
our path beset by muddy fate.
Trail footing slip'pry, frail, and fed—
and soon the pesky skeeter came.

>i< it's feeding time,
the first one's mine >i<

The day was calm, the sun shone bright,
dark fragrant earth smelled rainfall fresh.
All verdant green this time of year.
"Ahah!" a doe and fawn in crèche,
A perfect day, save 'wing-ed' fear—
Again—I heard mosquito's flight.

>i< prost, to your health,
proceed with stealth >i<

Ahead a bit in dappled light,
flowed woodland spring in fern-filled glen,
where sleek smooth stones gleamed rich like gems.
"My bug spray? Darn! Still sits in car.
To turn back now we've gone too far—
I think I felt mosquito's bite?"

>i< attack! attack!
they may turn back >i<

A phantom touch—a blade of grass?
A blood spot fresh upon my arm.
Like tiny jets, they dove en masse.
We turned our tails, full tilt, alarm'd
and saw the sign upon return,
its message gave us quite a turn—

ABANDON HOPE ALL TREKKERS HERE.
MOSQUITOES DRAIN YOUR HEART OF CHEER

Snow Spell

*

A snow day
Lightly blow day
A take it slow day

**

A meek day
Formless bleak day
Out window peek day

***

Book read day
Unmade bed day
A lightly tread day

****

Plans cede day
Deadlines freed day
Some dough to knead day

*****

Nap take day
Clock forsake day
A routine break day

******

Blue dirge day
Clutter purge day
Doldrums emerge day

****

Dense sky day
You and I day
To breathe and sigh day

The Hollowing

Ancient as the seasons,
it sits and waits on a windfall
with a soldier's indifference,
certain of victory before battle
in an asymmetrical conflict,
silent frostless breaths.
Watching with its wolf eyes—
ruthlessly—
though without knife or pistol,
only with its presence
for the combatant prey.
I begin my half-mile trek
through frozen woodland
in predawn graylight.
Slow soft stepping—
methodically—
so as not to waken a twig,
or a brittle leaf,
or a malevolent intent,
with a crack or snap.
To slink into my lair
without its notice.

It does not need to notice.
For it senses:
the scent of warmth,
the flavor of an intruder.
The frigidness advances,
iced and imperceptible—
And I shiver.
Seeping through thermal layers,
piercing warmth slowly,
the ache presses inward,
claiming appendages, torso, then vitals.

Finally, thoughts retreat to synapses,
like mid-winter sap to tree roots.
In staccato my teeth tremble—
dry leaves in gusty wind.
This cold—thief of my spirit

with its pickpocket touch
and knowing smile
surveys my hollowed shell,
the junkie craving a heat fix.
Surrendering, I flee to shelter—
Nature's cold-blooded victory complete.

Halfway Lake, Upper Peninsula

A black spiral notebook sprawls askew in my lap—
My pen dithering between fingers and thumb.
Its ink meanders slowly along pathways of thought,
its pattern as abstract as Halfway's surface swirls.

A portable dock below me, a breakfast beer by my feet—
never wanting to leave my aluminum-and-vinyl webbed nest.
Halfway between water and shore, halfway through vacation,
above the bridge, amid the great Superior and Michigan.

The shoreline jags and juts ungroomed and natural—
Balsam and pines knot and twist along the perimeter,
their tips desperately grasping toward the pure blue
as their green reflections fracture on the water's surface.

Scents of forest and lake rise as incense of amnesia,
causing words of the office to unravel, then dissolve.
The breeze teems with stories and poems unwritten,
as birds sing hymns to the lore of Hemingway.

How lovely the croak of the frog and the cry of the loon—
Their calls punctuate nature's verses of silence,
as great amens in a prayer of thanks—
for swaying reeds, pristine water, and darting minnows.

Innocently, the morning sun and clouds play hide-and-seek.
Their giddiness awakens the calm, which yawns and stretches.
Then rubs its eyes and returns to its muted slumber.
Amused, the lake skip-dances with tiny pirouettes of delight.

These gleanings will return with me to the city,
drafted, edited, digitized—domesticated.
Muses don't domesticate—they inspire.
Evoking from places like Halfway Lake.

November Farewell

On a drab November dawn
Clustered poplars stand stooped and bare—
Twisted limbs and gnarled hands upraised,
Swaying to a cantoring wind:
In Kaddish for the summer passed.

Pressed Leaf

To pen—
Avoiding the esoteric,
Instead embracing the power
Of witnessed indignation,
Without remedy yet rich in hope;
Forsaking the grand in metaphor or vision,
Seeking, clearly seeing the small and still;
Always, let it be with joy,
In the name of art, and for the sake of beauty.
But silently for me:
Truth in the moment; truth for the moment—
A pressed leaf in a book.

Stan Winarski's compass points to the Blue Hills of Northwest Wisconsin. This quiet landscape has been his source of inspiration, where lifelong connection to the natural world shapes his poetry. His work has appeared in *Solitary Plover, Bramble, The Wisconsin Fellowship of Poets Calendars*, and as spoken word on WDRT FM's The Landward Series. Selected from over 350 entries in the 2025 Finishing Line Press Open Chapbook Competition and winner of the 2026 Wisconsin Fellowship of Poets Muse Prize, he spent decades writing while balancing corporate work and family life. Now retired, he continues to find in these woodlands a silence that teaches and the accumulated wisdom that provides a centering no office ever could. He lives in Metro Milwaukee with his wife, Mary Kay, and has two adult children.

www.ingramcontent.com/pod-product-compliance
Lightning Source LLC
LaVergne TN
LVHW090541110826
845146LV00003B/1210

* 9 7 9 8 8 9 9 9 0 4 8 6 8 *